MznLnx

Missing Links Exam Preps

Exam Prep for

Prealgebra

McKeague, 4th Edition

The MznLnx Exam Prep is your link from the texbook and lecture to your exams.
The MznLnx Exam Preps are unauthorized and comprehensive reviews of your textbooks.

All material provided by MznLnx and Rico Publications (c) 2010
Textbook publishers and textbook authors do not particpate in or contribute to these reviews.

MznLnx

Rico
Publications

Exam Prep for Prealgebra
4th Edition
McKeague

Publisher: Raymond Houge
Assistant Editor: Michael Rouger
Text and Cover Designer: Lisa Buckner
Marketing Manager: Sara Swagger
Project Manager, Editorial Production: Jerry Emerson
Art Director: Vernon Lowerui

Product Manager: Dave Mason
Editorial Assitant: Rachel Guzmanji
Pedagogy: Debra Long
Cover Image: Jim Reed/Getty Images
Text and Cover Printer: City Printing, Inc.
Compositor: Media Mix, Inc.

(c) 2010 Rico Publications

ALL RIGHTS RESERVED. No part of this work covered by the copyright may be reproduced or used in any form or by an means--graphic, electronic, or mechanical, including photocopying, recording, taping, Web distribution, information storage, and retrieval systems, or in any other manner--without the written permission of the publisher.

Printed in the United States
ISBN:

For more information about our products, contact us at:
Dave.Mason@RicoPublications.com

For permission to use material from this text or product, submit a request online to:
Dave.Mason@RicoPublications.com

Contents

CHAPTER 1
Basic Properties and Definitions — 1

CHAPTER 2
Equations and Inequalities in One Variable — 18

CHAPTER 3
Equations and Inequalities in Two Variables — 25

CHAPTER 4
Systems of Linear Equations and Inequalities — 36

CHAPTER 5
Exponents and Polynomials — 39

CHAPTER 6
Rational Expressions and Rational Functions — 47

CHAPTER 7
Rational Exponents and Roots — 52

CHAPTER 8
Quadratic Functions — 59

CHAPTER 9
Exponential and Logarithmic Functions — 64

CHAPTER 10
Conic Sections — 71

ANSWER KEY — 75

TO THE STUDENT

COMPREHENSIVE

The *MznLnx* Exam Prep series is designed to help you pass your exams. Editors at MznLnx review your textbooks and then prepare these practice exams to help you master the textbook material. Unlike study guides, workbooks, and practice tests provided by the texbook publisher and textbook authors, *MznLnx* gives you **all** of the material in each chapter in exam form, not just samples, so you can be sure to nail your exam.

MECHANICAL

The MznLnx Exam Prep series creates exams that will help you learn the subject matter as well as test you on your understanding. Each question is designed to help you master the concept. Just working through the exams, you gain an understanding of the subject--its a simple mechanical process that produces success.

INTEGRATED STUDY GUIDE AND REVIEW

MznLnx is not just a set of exams designed to test you, its also a comprehensive review of the subject content. Each exam question is also a review of the concept, making sure that you will get the answer correct without having to go to other sources of material. You learn as you go! Its the easiest way to pass an exam.

HUMOR

Studying can be tedious and dry. MznLnx's instructional design includes moderate humor within the exam questions on occassion, to break the tedium and revitalize the brain

Chapter 1. Basic Properties and Definitions

1. The _____ of a quantity whose value decreases with time is the interval required for the quantity to decay to half of its initial value. The concept originated in describing how long it takes atoms to undergo radioactive decay, but also applies in a wide variety of other situations.

The term '_____' dates to 1907.

   a. 120-cell
   b. 1-center problem
   c. Half-life
   d. Radioactive decay

2. Leonardo of Pisa (c. 1170 - c. 1250), also known as Leonardo Pisano, Leonardo Bonacci, Leonardo _____, or, most commonly, simply _____, was an Italian mathematician, considered by some 'the most talented mathematician of the Middle Ages'.
   a. Harry Hinsley
   b. Fibonacci
   c. Ralph C. Merkle
   d. Guido Castelnuovo

3. A _____ or bar graph is a chart with rectangular bars with lengths proportional to the values that they represent. _____s are used for comparing two or more values. The bars can be horizontally or vertically oriented.
   a. 1-center problem
   b. Bar chart
   c. 2-3 heap
   d. 120-cell

4. In mathematics and computer science, _____ (also base-16, hexa or base, of 16. It uses sixteen distinct symbols, most often the symbols 0-9 to represent values zero to nine, and A, B, C, D, E, F (or a through f) to represent values ten to fifteen.

Its primary use is as a human friendly representation of binary coded values, so it is often used in digital electronics and computer engineering.

   a. Radix
   b. Tetradecimal
   c. Factoradic
   d. Hexadecimal

5. _____ is simply the manner of writing out an expression in full. When a quantity is written as a sum of terms, or as a continued product, _____ notation is used to illustrate the expression in its entirety.
   a. Algebraic element
   b. Algebra
   c. Algebraic function
   d. Expanded form

6. Exponentiation is a mathematical operation, written a^n, involving two numbers, the base a and the _____ n. When n is a positive integer, exponentiation corresponds to repeated multiplication:

$$a^n = \underbrace{a \times \cdots \times a}_{n},$$

just as multiplication by a positive integer corresponds to repeated addition:

$$a \times n = \underbrace{a + \cdots + a}_{n}.$$

The _____ is usually shown as a superscript to the right of the base. The exponentiation a^n can be read as: a raised to the n-th power, a raised to the power [of] n or possibly a raised to the _____ [of] n, or more briefly: a to the n-th power or a to the power [of] n, or even more briefly: a to the n.

   a. Exponent
   b. Exponentiating by squaring
   c. Exponential sum
   d. Exponential tree

7. In mathematics, a _____ is the end result of a division problem. It can also be expressed as the number of times the divisor divides into the dividend.
   a. Limiting
   b. Marginal cost
   c. Notation
   d. Quotient

Chapter 1. Basic Properties and Definitions 3

8. In mathematics, an _____ in the sense of ring theory is a subring $\mathcal{O}$ of a ring R that satisfies the conditions

   1. R is a ring which is a finite-dimensional algebra over the rational number field $\mathbb{Q}$
   2. $\mathcal{O}$ spans R over $\mathbb{Q}$, so that $\mathbb{Q}\mathcal{O} = R$, and
   3. $\mathcal{O}$ is a lattice in R.

The third condition can be stated more accurately, in terms of the extension of scalars of R to the real numbers, embedding R in a real vector space. In less formal terms, additively $\mathcal{O}$ should be a free abelian group generated by a basis for R over $\mathbb{Q}$.

The leading example is the case where R is a number field K and $\mathcal{O}$ is its ring of integers. In algebraic number theory there are examples for any K other than the rational field of proper subrings of the ring of integers that are also _____s.

   a. Efficiency
   b. Annihilator
   c. Algebraic
   d. Order

9. In algebra and computer programming, when a number or expression is both preceded and followed by a binary operation, a rule is required for which operation should be applied first; this rule is known as an _____ . From the earliest use of mathematical notation, multiplication took precedence over addition, whichever side of a number it appeared on. Thus 3 + 4 × 5 = 5 × 4 + 3 = 23.

   a. Algebraic K-theory
   b. Isomorphism class
   c. Identity element
   d. Order of operations

10. In mathematics, an _____ or member of a set is any one of the distinct objects that make up that set.

Writing A = {1,2,3,4}, means that the _____s of the set A are the numbers 1, 2, 3 and 4. Groups of _____s of A, for example {1,2}, are subsets of A.

   a. Order
   b. Universal code
   c. Ideal
   d. Element

11. In mathematics, especially in set theory, a set A is a _____ of a set B if A is 'contained' inside B. Notice that A and B may coincide. The relationship of one set being a _____ of another is called inclusion.
   a. Set of all sets
   b. Cartesian product
   c. Horizontal line test
   d. Subset

12. In mathematics, and more specifically set theory, the _____ is the unique set having no members. Some axiomatic set theories assure that the _____ exists by including an axiom of _____; in other theories, its existence can be deduced. Many possible properties of sets are trivially true for the _____.
   a. A Mathematical Theory of Communication
   b. Inverse function
   c. Empty function
   d. Empty set

13. In mathematics, the _____ of two sets A and B is the set that contains all elements of A that also belong to B, but no other elements.

For explanation of the symbols used in this article, refer to the table of mathematical symbols.

The _____ of A and B

The _____ of A and B is written 'A ∩ B'. Formally:

> x is an element of A ∩ B if and only if
> - x is an element of A and
> - x is an element of B.
>
> For example:
> - The _____ of the sets {1, 2, 3} and {2, 3, 4} is {2, 3}.
> - The number 9 is not in the _____ of the set of prime numbers {2, 3, 5, 7, 11, …} and the set of odd numbers {1, 3, 5, 7, 9, 11, …}.

If the _____ of two sets A and B is empty, that is they have no elements in common, then they are said to be disjoint, denoted: A ∩ B = ∅. For example the sets {1, 2} and {3, 4} are disjoint, written {1, 2} ∩ {3, 4} = ∅.

a. Order
b. Erlang
c. Advice
d. Intersection

14. In mathematics, a _____ is a set that is negligible in some sense. For different applications, the meaning of 'negligible' varies. In measure theory, any set of measure 0 is called a _____.
   a. Radonifying function
   b. Borel-Cantelli lemma
   c. Null set
   d. Prevalence and shyness

15. In set theory, the term _____ refers to a set operation used in the convergence of set elements to form a resultant set containing the elements of both sets. As a simple example, a _____ of two disjoint sets, which do not have elements in common results in a set containing all elements from both sets. A Venn diagram representing the _____ of sets A and B.
   a. UES
   b. Introduction
   c. Event
   d. Union

16. _____ or set diagrams are diagrams that show all hypothetically possible logical relations between a finite collection of sets. _____ were invented around 1880 by John Venn. They are used in many fields, including set theory, probability, logic, statistics, and computer science.
   a. Venn diagrams
   b. 2-3 heap
   c. 120-cell
   d. 1-center problem

17. A _____ is a 2D geometric symbolic representation of information according to some visualization technique. Sometimes, the technique uses a 3D visualization which is then projected onto the 2D surface. The word graph is sometimes used as a synonym for _____.
   a. 1-center problem
   b. 2-3 heap
   c. 120-cell
   d. Diagram

Chapter 1. Basic Properties and Definitions

18. In mathematics, a _____ is a statement that can be proved on the basis of explicitly stated or previously agreed assumptions.
   a. Theorem
   b. Disjunction introduction
   c. Boolean function
   d. Logical value

19. In mathematics, an _____ is a statement about the relative size or order of two objects, or about whether they are the same or not

- The notation a < b means that a is less than b.
- The notation a > b means that a is greater than b.
- The notation a ≠ b means that a is not equal to b, but does not say that one is bigger than the other or even that they can be compared in size.

In all these cases, a is not equal to b, hence, '_____'.

These relations are known as strict _____

- The notation a ≤ b means that a is less than or equal to b;
- The notation a ≥ b means that a is greater than or equal to b;

An additional use of the notation is to show that one quantity is much greater than another, normally by several orders of magnitude.

- The notation a << b means that a is much less than b.
- The notation a >> b means that a is much greater than b.

If the sense of the _____ is the same for all values of the variables for which its members are defined, then the _____ is called an 'absolute' or 'unconditional' _____. If the sense of an _____ holds only for certain values of the variables involved, but is reversed or destroyed for other values of the variables, it is called a conditional _____.

An _____ may appear unsolvable because it only states whether a number is larger or smaller than another number; but it is possible to apply the same operations for equalities to inequalities. For example, to find x for the _____ 10x > 23 one would divide 23 by 10.

   a. A Mathematical Theory of Communication
   b. Inequality
   c. A chemical equation
   d. A posteriori

Chapter 1. Basic Properties and Definitions

20. In mathematics, a _____ is a picture of a straight line in which the integers are shown as specially-marked points evenly spaced on the line. Although this image only shows the integers from -9 to 9, the line includes all real numbers, continuing 'forever' in each direction. It is often used as an aid in teaching simple addition and subtraction, especially involving negative numbers.
    a. Real number
    b. Point plotting
    c. Number line
    d. Number system

21. In mathematics, the _____ of a Euclidean space is a special point, usually denoted by the letter O, used as a fixed point of reference for the geometry of the surrounding space. In a Cartesian coordinate system, the _____ is the point where the axes of the system intersect. In Euclidean geometry, the _____ may be chosen freely as any convenient point of reference.
    a. Interval
    b. OMAC
    c. Autonomous system
    d. Origin

22. In mathematics, the _____s may be described informally in several different ways. The _____s include both rational numbers, such as 42 and −23/129, and irrational numbers, such as pi and the square root of two; or, a _____ can be given by an infinite decimal representation, such as 2.4871773339...., where the digits continue in some way; or, the _____s may be thought of as points on an infinitely long number line.

    These descriptions of the _____s, while intuitively accessible, are not sufficiently rigorous for the purposes of pure mathematics.

    a. Minkowski distance
    b. Real number
    c. Pre-algebra
    d. Tally marks

23. In mathematics, the _____ of a real number is its numerical value without regard to its sign. So, for example, 3 is the _____ of both 3 and −3.

    The _____ of a number a is denoted by $|a|$.

    Generalizations of the _____ for real numbers occur in a wide variety of mathematical settings.

Chapter 1. Basic Properties and Definitions

a. A Mathematical Theory of Communication
b. A chemical equation
c. Area hyperbolic functions
d. Absolute value

24. A _____ is a simple shape of Euclidean geometry consisting of those points in a plane which are at a constant distance, called the radius, from a fixed point, called the center. A _____ with center A is sometimes denoted by the symbol A.

A chord of a _____ is a line segment whose two endpoints lie on the _____.

a. Circumcircle
b. Malfatti circles
c. Circular segment
d. Circle

25. In mathematics, a _____ can mean either an element of the set {1, 2, 3, ...} or an element of the set {0, 1, 2, 3, ...}. The latter is especially preferred in mathematical logic, set theory, and computer science.

_____s have two main purposes: they can be used for counting, and they can be used for ordering.

a. Strong partition cardinal
b. Cardinal numbers
c. Suslin cardinal
d. Natural number

26. The _____ are the set of numbers consisting of the natural numbers including 0 and their negatives. They are numbers that can be written without a fractional or decimal component, and fall within the set {... −2, −1, 0, 1, 2, ...}.
a. A chemical equation
b. A posteriori
c. A Mathematical Theory of Communication
d. Integers

27. In mathematics, a _____ is a number which can be expressed as a ratio of two integers. Non-integer _____s are usually written as the vulgar fraction $\frac{a}{b}$, where b is not zero. a is called the numerator, and b the denominator.

Chapter 1. Basic Properties and Definitions 9

   a. Tally marks
   b. Minkowski distance
   c. Pre-algebra
   d. Rational number

28. In mathematics, a _____ can mean either an element of the set {1, 2, 3, ...} (i.e the positive integers) or an element of the set {0, 1, 2, 3, ...} (i.e. the non-negative integers).
   a. FISH
   b. Bounded
   c. Degrees of freedom
   d. Whole number

29. A _____ number is a positive integer which has a positive divisor other than one or itself. By definition, every integer greater than one is either a prime number or a _____ number.zero and one are considered to be neither prime nor _____. For example, the integer 14 is a _____ number because it can be factored as 2 × 7.
   a. Composite
   b. Discontinuity
   c. Key server
   d. Basis

30. A _____ is a positive integer which has a positive divisor other than one or itself. In other words, if 0 < n is an integer and there are integers 1 < a, b < n such that n = a × b then n is composite. By definition, every integer greater than one is either a prime number or a _____.
   a. Megaprime
   b. Ruth-Aaron pair
   c. Prime Pages
   d. Composite number

31. In mathematics, a _____ is a natural number which has exactly two distinct natural number divisors: 1 and itself. An infinitude of _____s exists, as demonstrated by Euclid around 300 BC. The first twenty-five _____s are:

   2, 3, 5, 7, 11, 13, 17, 19, 23, 29, 31, 37, 41, 43, 47, 53, 59, 61, 67, 71, 73, 79, 83, 89, 97.

a. Pronic number
b. Highly composite number
c. Perrin number
d. Prime number

32. In mathematics, a _____ is a mathematical statement which appears resourceful, but has not been formally proven to be true under the rules of mathematical logic. Once a _____ is formally proven true it is elevated to the status of theorem and may be used afterwards without risk in the construction of other formal mathematical proofs. Until that time, mathematicians may use the _____ on a provisional basis, but any resulting work is itself provisional until the underlying _____ is cleared up.

a. Conjecture
b. Heawood conjecture
c. Whitehead conjecture
d. Moral certainty

33. In mathematics, the _____ of a non-negative integer n, denoted by n!, is the product of all positive integers less than or equal to n. For example,

$$5! = 1 \times 2 \times 3 \times 4 \times 5 = 120$$

and
$$6! = 1 \times 2 \times 3 \times 4 \times 5 \times 6 = 720$$

The notation n! was introduced by Christian Kramp in 1808.

The _____ function is formally defined by

$$n! = \prod_{k=1}^{n} k \qquad \forall n \in \mathbb{N}.$$

The above definition incorporates the instance

$$0! = 1$$

as an instance of the fact that the product of no numbers at all is 1.

Chapter 1. Basic Properties and Definitions

a. Partition of a set
b. Factorial
c. Symbolic combinatorics
d. Plane partition

34. In mathematics, in the realm of group theory, a group is said to be _____ if it equals its own commutator subgroup if the group has no nontrivial abelian quotients.

The smallest _____ group is the alternating group A_5. More generally, any non-abelian simple group is _____ since the commutator subgroup is a normal subgroup with abelian quotient.

a. Group of Lie type
b. Quaternion group
c. Free product
d. Perfect

35. In mathematics, a _____ is defined as a positive integer which is the sum of its proper positive divisors, that is, the sum of the positive divisors excluding the number itself. Equivalently, a _____ is a number that is half the sum of all of its positive divisors, or = 2n.

The first _____ is 6, because 1, 2, and 3 are its proper positive divisors, and 1 + 2 + 3 = 6.

a. Leonardo numbers
b. Blum integer
c. Nonhypotenuse number
d. Perfect number

36. In set theory, a _____ is a partially ordered set such that for each t ∈ T, the set {s ∈ T : s < t} is well-ordered by the relation <. For each t ∈ T, the order type of {s ∈ T : s < t} is called the height of t. The height of T itself is the least ordinal greater than the height of each element of T.

a. Set-theoretic topology
b. Definable numbers
c. Tree
d. Transitive reduction

37. In mathematics, the _____ of a number n is the number that, when added to n, yields zero. The _____ of n is denoted −n. For example, 7 is −7, because 7 + (−7) = 0, and the _____ of −0.3 is 0.3, because −0.3 + 0.3 = 0.

a. Algebraic structure
b. Additive inverse
c. Associativity
d. Arity

38. In mathematics, and in particular in abstract algebra, distributivity is a property of binary operations that generalises the _____ law from elementary algebra.
    a. General linear group
    b. Permutation
    c. Closure with a twist
    d. Distributive

39. _____ is the mathematical operation of scaling one number by another. It is one of the four basic operations in elementary arithmetic.

_____ is defined for whole numbers in terms of repeated addition; for example, 4 multiplied by 3 can be calculated by adding 3 copies of 4 together:

$$4 + 4 + 4 = 12.$$

_____ of rational numbers and real numbers is defined by systematic generalization of this basic idea.

a. Multiplication
b. Least common multiple
c. Highest common factor
d. The number 0 is even.

40. In elementary algebra, a _____ is a polynomial with two terms: the sum of two monomials. It is the simplest kind of polynomial except for a monomial.

The _____ $a^2 - b^2$ can be factored as the product of two other _____ s:

$a^2 - b^2$.

The product of a pair of linear _____ s a x + b and c x + d is:

2 +x + bd.

Chapter 1. Basic Properties and Definitions 13

A _____ raised to the nth power, represented as

n

can be expanded by means of the _____ theorem or, equivalently, using Pascal's triangle.

   a. Cylindrical algebraic decomposition
   b. Rational root theorem
   c. Binomial
   d. Real structure

41. In mathematics, a _____ for a number x, denoted by $1/x$ or x^{-1}, is a number which when multiplied by x yields the multiplicative identity, 1. The _____ of x is also called the reciprocal of x. The _____ of a fraction p/q is q/p.
   a. Double exponential
   b. Golden function
   c. Hyperbolic function
   d. Multiplicative inverse

42. In mathematics, the multiplicative inverse of a number x, denoted $1/x$ or x^{-1}, is the number which, when multiplied by x, yields 1. The multiplicative inverse of x is also called the _____ of x.
   a. 2-3 heap
   b. 120-cell
   c. 1-center problem
   d. Reciprocal

43. In mathematics, _____ is a property that a binary operation can have. It means that, within an expression containing two or more of the same associative operators in a row, the order that the operations are performed does not matter as long as the sequence of the operands is not changed. That is, rearranging the parentheses in such an expression will not change its value.
   a. Unital
   b. Algebraically closed
   c. Associativity
   d. Idempotence

44. In mathematics, the _____ or least common denominator is the least common multiple of the denominators of a set of vulgar fractions. It is the smallest positive integer that is a multiple of the denominators. For instance, the _____ of

$$\left\{\frac{5}{12}, \frac{11}{18}\right\}$$

is 36 because the least common multiple of 12 and 18 is 36.

   a. The number 0 is even.
   b. Highest common factor
   c. Subtrahend
   d. Lowest common denominator

45. In linear algebra, two n-by-n matrices A and B over the field K are called _____ if there exists an invertible n-by-n matrix P over K such that

$$P^{-1}AP = B.$$

One of the meanings of the term similarity transformation is such a transformation of a matrix A into a matrix B.

Similarity is an equivalence relation on the space of square matrices.

_____ matrices share many properties:

- rank
- determinant
- trace
- eigenvalues
- characteristic polynomial
- minimal polynomial
- elementary divisors

There are two reasons for these facts:

- two _____ matrices can be thought of as describing the same linear map, but with respect to different bases
- the map $X \mapsto P^{-1}XP$ is an automorphism of the associative algebra of all n-by-n matrices, as the one-object case of the above category of all matrices.

Because of this, for a given matrix A, one is interested in finding a simple 'normal form' B which is _____ to A -- the study of A then reduces to the study of the simpler matrix B.

Chapter 1. Basic Properties and Definitions   15

   a. Coherence
   b. Dense
   c. Blinding
   d. Similar

46. In mathematics, the _____s are an extension of the real numbers obtained by adjoining an imaginary unit, denoted i, which satisfies:

$$i^2 = -1.$$

Every _____ can be written in the form a + bi, where a and b are real numbers called the real part and the imaginary part of the _____, respectively.

_____s are a field, and thus have addition, subtraction, multiplication, and division operations. These operations extend the corresponding operations on real numbers, although with a number of additional elegant and useful properties, e.g., negative real numbers can be obtained by squaring _____s.

   a. Real part
   b. 1-center problem
   c. 120-cell
   d. Complex number

47. In mathematics the _____ of a set which is equipped with the operation of addition is an element which, when added to any element x in the set, yields x. One of the most familiar additive identities is the number 0 from elementary mathematics, but additive identities occur in other mathematical structures where addition is defined, such as in groups and rings.

- The _____ familiar from elementary mathematics is zero, denoted 0. For example,

   5 + 0 = 5 = 0 + 5.

- In the natural numbers N and all of its supersets, the _____ is 0. Thus for any one of these numbers n,

   n + 0 = n = 0 + n.

Let N be a set which is closed under the operation of addition, denoted +. An _____ for N is any element e such that for any element n in N,

   e + n = n = n + e.

a. Unit ring
b. Additive identity
c. Algebraically independent
d. Unique factorization domain

48. In mathematics, the term _____ has several different important meanings:

- An _____ is an equality that remains true regardless of the values of any variables that appear within it, to distinguish it from an equality which is true under more particular conditions. For this, the 'triple bar' symbol ≡ is sometimes used.
- In algebra, an _____ or _____ element of a set S with a binary operation Â· is an element e that, when combined with any element x of S, produces that same x. That is, eÂ·x = xÂ·e = x for all x in S.
    - The _____ function from a set S to itself, often denoted id or id_S, s the function such that i = x for all x in S. This function serves as the _____ element in the set of all functions from S to itself with respect to function composition.
    - In linear algebra, the _____ matrix of size n is the n-by-n square matrix with ones on the main diagonal and zeros elsewhere. This matrix serves as the _____ with respect to matrix multiplication.

A common example of the first meaning is the trigonometric _____

$$\sin^2 \theta + \cos^2 \theta = 1$$

which is true for all real values of θ, as opposed to

$$\cos \theta = 1,$$

which is true only for some values of θ, not all. For example, the latter equation is true when $\theta = 0$, false when $\theta = 2$

The concepts of 'additive _____' and 'multiplicative _____' are central to the Peano axioms. The number 0 is the 'additive _____' for integers, real numbers, and complex numbers. For the real numbers, for all $a \in \mathbb{R}$,

$$0 + a = a,$$
$$a + 0 = a, \text{ and}$$
$$0 + 0 = 0.$$

Similarly, The number 1 is the 'multiplicative _____' for integers, real numbers, and complex numbers.

Chapter 1. Basic Properties and Definitions

a. Intersection
b. ARIA
c. Identity
d. Action

49. In mathematics, an arithmetic progression or _____ is a sequence of numbers such that the difference of any two successive members of the sequence is a constant. For instance, the sequence 3, 5, 7, 9, 11, 13... is an arithmetic progression with common difference 2.
   a. Arithmetic sequence
   b. Edgeworth series
   c. Eisenstein series
   d. Alternating series test

50. Induction or _____, sometimes called inductive logic, is the process of reasoning in which the premises of an argument are believed to support the conclusion but do not entail it;. Induction is a form of reasoning that makes generalizations based on individual instances. It is used to ascribe properties or relations to types based on an observation instance; or to formulate laws based on limited observations of recurring phenomenal patterns.
   a. Intuitionistic logic
   b. Inductive reasoning
   c. Affine logic
   d. Idempotency of entailment

51. In a graph theory, the _____ L

One of the earliest and most important theorems about _____s is due to Hassler Whitney, who proved that with one exceptional case the structure of G can be recovered completely from its _____.

   a. Vertex-transitive graph
   b. Line graph
   c. Sparse graph
   d. Bivariegated graph

Chapter 2. Equations and Inequalities in One Variable

1. A _____ is an algebraic equation in which each term is either a constant or the product of a constant and a single variable. _____s can have one, two, three or more variables.

   _____s occur with great regularity in applied mathematics.

   a. Quadratic equation
   b. Difference of two squares
   c. Quartic equation
   d. Linear equation

2. In mathematics, the _____ of a real number is its numerical value without regard to its sign. So, for example, 3 is the _____ of both 3 and −3.

   The _____ of a number a is denoted by $|a|$.

   Generalizations of the _____ for real numbers occur in a wide variety of mathematical settings.

   a. Area hyperbolic functions
   b. A chemical equation
   c. A Mathematical Theory of Communication
   d. Absolute value

3. In the study of metric spaces in mathematics, there are various notions of two metrics on the same underlying space being 'the same', or _____.

   In the following, M will denote a non-empty set and d_1 and d_2 will denote two metrics on M.

   The two metrics d_1 and d_2 are said to be topologically _____ if they generate the same topology on M.

   a. A chemical equation
   b. A Mathematical Theory of Communication
   c. A posteriori
   d. Equivalent

4. _____ is the mathematical operation of scaling one number by another. It is one of the four basic operations in elementary arithmetic.

_____ is defined for whole numbers in terms of repeated addition; for example, 4 multiplied by 3 can be calculated by adding 3 copies of 4 together:

$$4 + 4 + 4 = 12.$$

_____ of rational numbers and real numbers is defined by systematic generalization of this basic idea.

a. The number 0 is even.
b. Least common multiple
c. Highest common factor
d. Multiplication

5. In mathematics, the _____ of a polynomial is the term of degree 0. For example, in the polynomial

X³ + 2X + 3

over the variable X, the _____ is 3. Here, the _____ is given by a numeral, but it may also be specified by a letter that is a parameter rather than a variable, as in the polynomial

ax² + bx + c,

in the variable x, where a, b, and c are parameters so that c is the _____.

a. Stability radius
b. Jacobian conjecture
c. Sheffer sequence
d. Constant term

6. In mathematics and in the sciences, a _____ (plural: _____e, formulæ or _____s) is a concise way of expressing information symbolically (as in a mathematical or chemical _____), or a general relationship between quantities. One of many famous _____e is Albert Einstein's E = mc² (see special relativity)

In mathematics, a _____ is a key to solve an equation with variables. For example, the problem of determining the volume of a sphere is one that requires a significant amount of integral calculus to solve.

Chapter 2. Equations and Inequalities in One Variable

a. Formula
b. 120-cell
c. 2-3 heap
d. 1-center problem

7. _____ is a quantity expressing the two-dimensional size of a defined part of a surface, typically a region bounded by a closed curve. The term surface _____ refers to the total _____ of the exposed surface of a 3-dimensional solid, such as the sum of the _____s of the exposed sides of a polyhedron. _____ is an important invariant in the differential geometry of surfaces.
   a. A posteriori
   b. A chemical equation
   c. Area
   d. A Mathematical Theory of Communication

8. The _____ is the length of the line that bounds an area In the special case where the area is circular, the _____ is known as the circumference.
   a. Perimeter
   b. Reflection symmetry
   c. Multilateration
   d. Concyclic

9. In calculus, a function f defined on a subset of the real numbers with real values is called monotonic (also monotonically increasing or non-_____), if for all x and y such that x ≤ y one has f(x) ≤ f(y), so f preserves the order. In layman's terms, the sign of the slope is always positive (the curve tending upwards) or zero (i.e., non-_____, or asymptotic, or depicted as a horizontal, flat line) Likewise, a function is called monotonically _____ (non-increasing) if, whenever x ≤ y, then f(x) ≥ f(y), so it reverses the order.
   a. Dual pair
   b. Circular convolution
   c. Tensor product of Hilbert spaces
   d. Decreasing

10. Leonardo of Pisa (c. 1170 - c. 1250), also known as Leonardo Pisano, Leonardo Bonacci, Leonardo _____, or, most commonly, simply _____, was an Italian mathematician, considered by some 'the most talented mathematician of the Middle Ages'.

a. Harry Hinsley
b. Guido Castelnuovo
c. Ralph C. Merkle
d. Fibonacci

11. In mathematics, a _____ is a statement that can be proved on the basis of explicitly stated or previously agreed assumptions.
    a. Disjunction introduction
    b. Boolean function
    c. Logical value
    d. Theorem

12. In geometry and trigonometry, an _____ is the figure formed by two rays sharing a common endpoint, called the vertex of the _____. The magnitude of the _____ is the 'amount of rotation' that separates the two rays, and can be measured by considering the length of circular arc swept out when one ray is rotated about the vertex to coincide with the other. Where there is no possibility of confusion, the term '_____' is used interchangeably for both the geometric configuration itself and for its angular magnitude.
    a. Angle
    b. A Mathematical Theory of Communication
    c. A posteriori
    d. A chemical equation

13. An angle smaller than a right angle is called an _____ (less than 90 degrees).
    a. Euclidean geometry
    b. Ultraparallel theorem
    c. Integral geometry
    d. Acute Angle

14. A pair of angles are complementary if the sum of their measures add up to 90 degrees.

If the two _____ are adjacent (i.e. have a common vertex and share a side, but do not have any interior points in common) their non-shared sides form a right angle.

In Euclidean geometry, the two acute angles in a right triangle are complementary, because there are 180>° in a triangle and 90>° have been accounted for by the right angle.

Chapter 2. Equations and Inequalities in One Variable

   a. Complementary Angles
   b. Quincunx
   c. Conway polyhedron notation
   d. Hypotenuse

15. In mathematics the concept of a _____ generalizes notions such as 'length', 'area', and 'volume'. Informally, given some base set, a '_____' is any consistent assignment of 'sizes' to the subsets of the base set. Depending on the application, the 'size' of a subset may be interpreted as its physical size, the amount of something that lies within the subset, or the probability that some random process will yield a result within the subset.
   a. Congruent
   b. Cusp
   c. Lattice
   d. Measure

16. In geometry and trigonometry, a _____ is defined as an angle between two straight intersecting lines of ninety degrees, or one-quarter of a circle.
   a. Right Angle
   b. Sine integral
   c. Trigonometry
   d. Trigonometric functions

17. An angle equal to two right angles is called a _____ (equal to 180 degrees).
   a. Theorem
   b. Straight Angle
   c. Householder transformation
   d. Loomis-Whitney inequality

18. A pair of angles is _____ if their measurements add up to 180 degrees. If the two _____ angles are adjacent their non-shared sides form a straight line. The supplement of 135 would be 45.
   a. Dense
   b. Supplementary
   c. FISH
   d. Cylinder

Chapter 2. Equations and Inequalities in One Variable   23

19. In set theory, a _____ is a partially ordered set such that for each t ∈ T, the set {s ∈ T : s < t} is well-ordered by the relation <. For each t ∈ T, the order type of {s ∈ T : s < t} is called the height of t. The height of T itself is the least ordinal greater than the height of each element of T.
   a. Tree
   b. Set-theoretic topology
   c. Transitive reduction
   d. Definable numbers

20. A _____ is a 2D geometric symbolic representation of information according to some visualization technique. Sometimes, the technique uses a 3D visualization which is then projected onto the 2D surface. The word graph is sometimes used as a synonym for _____.
   a. 2-3 heap
   b. 1-center problem
   c. 120-cell
   d. Diagram

21. In mathematics, an _____ is a statement about the relative size or order of two objects, or about whether they are the same or not

   - The notation a < b means that a is less than b.
   - The notation a > b means that a is greater than b.
   - The notation a ≠ b means that a is not equal to b, but does not say that one is bigger than the other or even that they can be compared in size.

In all these cases, a is not equal to b, hence, '_____'.

These relations are known as strict _____

   - The notation a ≤ b means that a is less than or equal to b;
   - The notation a ≥ b means that a is greater than or equal to b;

An additional use of the notation is to show that one quantity is much greater than another, normally by several orders of magnitude.

   - The notation a << b means that a is much less than b.
   - The notation a >> b means that a is much greater than b.

If the sense of the _____ is the same for all values of the variables for which its members are defined, then the _____ is called an 'absolute' or 'unconditional' _____. If the sense of an _____ holds only for certain values of the variables involved, but is reversed or destroyed for other values of the variables, it is called a conditional _____.

An _____ may appear unsolvable because it only states whether a number is larger or smaller than another number; but it is possible to apply the same operations for equalities to inequalities. For example, to find x for the _____ 10x > 23 one would divide 23 by 10.

   a. A posteriori
   b. A chemical equation
   c. A Mathematical Theory of Communication
   d. Inequality

22. A _____ is a simple shape of Euclidean geometry consisting of those points in a plane which are at a constant distance, called the radius, from a fixed point, called the center. A _____ with center A is sometimes denoted by the symbol A.

A chord of a _____ is a line segment whose two endpoints lie on the _____.

   a. Circumcircle
   b. Circular segment
   c. Circle
   d. Malfatti circles

23. In mathematics, a _____ is a set of real numbers with the property that any number that lies between two numbers in the set is also included in the set. For example, the set of all numbers x satisfying $0 \leq x \leq 1$ is an _____ which contains 0 and 1, as well as all numbers between them. Other examples of _____s are the set of all real numbers $\mathbb{R}$, the set of all positive real numbers, and the empty set.
   a. Annihilator
   b. Order
   c. Ideal
   d. Interval

24. _____ is the notation in which permitted values for a variable are expressed as ranging over a certain interval; "5 < x < 9" is an example of the application of _____.
   a. A Mathematical Theory of Communication
   b. Interval notation
   c. Infinity
   d. Implicit differentiation

Chapter 3. Equations and Inequalities in Two Variables

1. A _____ or bar graph is a chart with rectangular bars with lengths proportional to the values that they represent. _____s are used for comparing two or more values. The bars can be horizontally or vertically oriented.
   a. 2-3 heap
   b. Bar chart
   c. 1-center problem
   d. 120-cell

2. In a graph theory, the _____ L

   One of the earliest and most important theorems about _____s is due to Hassler Whitney, who proved that with one exceptional case the structure of G can be recovered completely from its _____.

   a. Vertex-transitive graph
   b. Bivariegated graph
   c. Line graph
   d. Sparse graph

3. In quantum field theory and statistical mechanics in the thermodynamic limit, a system with a global symmetry can have more than one phase. For parameters where the symmetry is spontaneously broken, the system is said to be _____. When the global symmetry is unbroken the system is disordered.
   a. Isoenthalpic-isobaric ensemble
   b. Ursell function
   c. Einstein relation
   d. Ordered

4. In mathematics, an _____ is a collection of objects having two coordinates (or entries or projections), such that one can always uniquely determine the object, which is the first coordinate (or first entry or left projection) of the pair as well as the second coordinate (or second entry or right projection.) If the first coordinate is a and the second is b, the usual notation for an _____ is (a, b.) The pair is 'ordered' in that (a, b) differs from (b, a) unless a = b.
   a. A posteriori
   b. Ordered pair
   c. A Mathematical Theory of Communication
   d. A chemical equation

5. The _____ is the horizontal axis of a two- dimensional plot in the Cartesian coordinate system, that is typically pointed to the right. Also known as a right-handed coordinate system.

Chapter 3. Equations and Inequalities in Two Variables

a. 2-3 heap
b. 1-center problem
c. 120-cell
d. X-axis

6. The _____ is one of the coordinates of a point in a two or three-dimensional cartesian coordinate system, equal to the distance of a point from the y-axis in a 2D system, or from the plane of y and z axes in a 3D system, measured along a line parallel to the x axis.
   a. X-coordinate
   b. 1-center problem
   c. 2-3 heap
   d. 120-cell

7. The _____ is the distance between a point and an axis in the Cartesian Coordinate System.
   a. 120-cell
   b. 1-center problem
   c. 2-3 heap
   d. Y-coordinate

8. The x-axis is the horizontal axis of a two-dimensional plot in the _____, that is typically pointed to the right. Also known as a right-handed coordinate system.
   a. 2-3 heap
   b. 1-center problem
   c. Cartesian coordinate system
   d. 120-cell

9. In mathematics, the _____ of a Euclidean space is a special point, usually denoted by the letter O, used as a fixed point of reference for the geometry of the surrounding space. In a Cartesian coordinate system, the _____ is the point where the axes of the system intersect. In Euclidean geometry, the _____ may be chosen freely as any convenient point of reference.
   a. Interval
   b. OMAC
   c. Autonomous system
   d. Origin

10. A _____ consists of one quarter of the coordinate plane.

a. 120-cell
b. 2-3 heap
c. 1-center problem
d. Quadrant

11. A _____ is a simple shape of Euclidean geometry consisting of those points in a plane which are at a constant distance, called the radius, from a fixed point, called the center. A _____ with center A is sometimes denoted by the symbol A.

A chord of a _____ is a line segment whose two endpoints lie on the _____.

a. Circular segment
b. Circle
c. Circumcircle
d. Malfatti circles

12. In reference to a 2D and 3D plane, the _____ is the vertical height of a 2D or 3D object.
a. 120-cell
b. 1-center problem
c. 2-3 heap
d. Y-axis

13. A _____ is an algebraic equation in which each term is either a constant or the product of a constant and a single variable. _____s can have one, two, three or more variables.

_____s occur with great regularity in applied mathematics.

a. Quadratic equation
b. Linear equation
c. Quartic equation
d. Difference of two squares

14. _____, also sometimes known as standard form or as exponential notation, is a way of writing numbers that accommodates values too large or small to be conveniently written in standard decimal notation. _____ has a number of useful properties and is often favored by scientists, mathematicians and engineers, who work with such numbers.

In _____, numbers are written in the form:

$$a \times 10^b$$

  a. Leading zero
  b. Radix point
  c. Scientific notation
  d. 1-center problem

15. In mathematics, the _____ of a real number is its numerical value without regard to its sign. So, for example, 3 is the _____ of both 3 and −3.

The _____ of a number a is denoted by $|a|$.

Generalizations of the _____ for real numbers occur in a wide variety of mathematical settings.

  a. A Mathematical Theory of Communication
  b. Area hyperbolic functions
  c. A chemical equation
  d. Absolute value

16. In mathematics, the _____s are an extension of the real numbers obtained by adjoining an imaginary unit, denoted i, which satisfies:

$$i^2 = -1.$$

Every _____ can be written in the form a + bi, where a and b are real numbers called the real part and the imaginary part of the _____, respectively.

_____s are a field, and thus have addition, subtraction, multiplication, and division operations. These operations extend the corresponding operations on real numbers, although with a number of additional elegant and useful properties, e.g., negative real numbers can be obtained by squaring _____s.

  a. Complex number
  b. 1-center problem
  c. Real part
  d. 120-cell

17. _____ is the study of geometry using the principles of algebra. That the algebra of the real numbers can be employed to yield results about the linear continuum of geometry relies on the Cantor-Dedekind axiom. Usually the Cartesian coordinate system is applied to manipulate equations for planes, straight lines, and squares, often in two and sometimes in three dimensions of measurement.

   a. Axis-aligned object
   b. Angular eccentricity
   c. Ambient space
   d. Analytic geometry

18. _____ is a part of mathematics concerned with questions of size, shape, and relative position of figures and with properties of space. _____ is one of the oldest sciences. Initially a body of practical knowledge concerning lengths, areas, and volumes, in the third century BC _____ was put into an axiomatic form by Euclid, whose treatment--Euclidean _____--set a standard for many centuries to follow.

   a. 1-center problem
   b. 120-cell
   c. 2-3 heap
   d. Geometry

19. A _____ is an opening in a wall that allows the passage of light and, if not closed or sealed, air and sound. _____s are usually glazed or covered in some other transparent or translucent material. _____s are held in place by frames, which prevent them from collapsing in.

   a. 1-center problem
   b. 2-3 heap
   c. 120-cell
   d. Window

20. In linear algebra, the _____ of an n-by-n square matrix A is defined to be the sum of the elements on the main diagonal of A. wikimedia.org/math/8/2/b/82be32fa00bd97ebbc066aec3dfe72da.png">

where a_{ij} represents the entry on the ith row and jth column of A. Equivalently, the _____ of a matrix is the sum of its eigenvalues, making it an invariant with respect to a change of basis.

   a. Lattice
   b. Constructivism
   c. Blinding
   d. Trace

Chapter 3. Equations and Inequalities in Two Variables

21. _____ is used to describe the steepness, incline, gradient, or grade of a straight line. A higher _____ value indicates a steeper incline. The _____ is defined as the ratio of the 'rise' divided by the 'run' between two points on a line, or in other words, the ratio of the altitude change to the horizontal distance between any two points on the line.
    a. Number line
    b. Point plotting
    c. Cognitively Guided Instruction
    d. Slope

22. A _____ of a curve is the envelope of a family of congruent circles centered on the curve. It generalises the concept of _____ lines.

    It is sometimes called the offset curve but the term 'offset' often refers also to translation.

    a. Cycloid
    b. Cissoid
    c. Parallel
    d. Bifolium

23. The existence and properties of _____ are the basis of Euclid's parallel postulate. _____ are two lines on the same plane that do not intersect even assuming that lines extend to infinity in either direction.
    a. Square wheel
    b. Vertical translation
    c. Spidron
    d. Parallel lines

24. In mathematics, the _____ is an approach to finding a particular solution to certain inhomogeneous ordinary differential equations and recurrence relations. It is closely related to the annihilator method, but instead of using a particular kind of differential operator in order to find the best possible form of the particular solution, a 'guess' is made as to the appropriate form, which is then tested by differentiating the resulting equation. In this sense, the _____ is less formal but more intuitive than the annihilator method.
    a. Linear differential equation
    b. Phase line
    c. Differential algebraic equations
    d. Method of undetermined coefficients

25. In statistics, the _____ problem occurs when one considers a set of statistical inferences simultaneously. Errors in inference, including confidence intervals that fail to include their corresponding population parameters are more likely when one considers the family as a whole.

Chapter 3. Equations and Inequalities in Two Variables

The term 'comparisons' in _____ typically refers to comparisons of two groups, such as treatment versus control.

a. Cross-validation
b. Multiple comparisons
c. Closed testing procedure
d. Familywise error rate

26. A _____ is a set of curves, each of which is given by a function or parametrization in which one or more of the parameters is variable. In general, the parameter(s) influence the shape of the curve in a way that is more complicated than a simple linear transformation. Sets of curves given by an implicit relation may also represent families of curves.
   a. Crystalline cohomology
   b. Regular local ring
   c. Quantum cohomology
   d. Family of curves

27. In mathematics, the concept of a _____ tries to capture the intuitive idea of a geometrical one-dimensional and continuous object. A simple example is the circle. In everyday use of the term '_____', a straight line is not curved, but in mathematical parlance _____s include straight lines and line segments.
   a. Kappa curve
   b. Quadrifolium
   c. Negative pedal curve
   d. Curve

28. _____ is a form where m is the slope of the line and b is the y-intercept, which is the y-coordinate of the point where the line crosses the y axis. This can be seen by letting x = 0, which immediately gives y = b.
   a. Separable extension
   b. Dynamical system
   c. Commutative law
   d. Slope-intercept form

29. The _____ expresses the fact that the difference in the y coordinate between two points on a line that is, y − y1 is proportional to the difference in the x coordinate that is, x − x1. The proportionality constant is m (the slope of the line.

a. Rubin Causal Model
b. Square function
c. Cobb-Douglas
d. Point-slope form

30. In topology, the _____ of a subset S of a topological space X is the set of points which can be approached both from S and from the outside of S. More formally, it is the set of points in the closure of S, not belonging to the interior of S. An element of the _____ of S is called a _____ point of S.
   a. Bertrand paradox
   b. Boundary
   c. Heap
   d. Character

31. In mathematics, an _____ is a statement about the relative size or order of two objects, or about whether they are the same or not

- The notation a < b means that a is less than b.
- The notation a > b means that a is greater than b.
- The notation a ≠ b means that a is not equal to b, but does not say that one is bigger than the other or even that they can be compared in size.

In all these cases, a is not equal to b, hence, '_____'.

These relations are known as strict _____

- The notation a ≤ b means that a is less than or equal to b;
- The notation a ≥ b means that a is greater than or equal to b;

An additional use of the notation is to show that one quantity is much greater than another, normally by several orders of magnitude.

- The notation a << b means that a is much less than b.
- The notation a >> b means that a is much greater than b.

If the sense of the _____ is the same for all values of the variables for which its members are defined, then the _____ is called an 'absolute' or 'unconditional' _____. If the sense of an _____ holds only for certain values of the variables involved, but is reversed or destroyed for other values of the variables, it is called a conditional _____.

Chapter 3. Equations and Inequalities in Two Variables

An _____ may appear unsolvable because it only states whether a number is larger or smaller than another number; but it is possible to apply the same operations for equalities to inequalities. For example, to find x for the _____ 10x > 23 one would divide 23 by 10.

a. Inequality
b. A chemical equation
c. A posteriori
d. A Mathematical Theory of Communication

32. The mathematical concept of a _____ expresses the intuitive idea of deterministic dependence between two quantities, one of which is viewed as primary and the other as secondary. A _____ then is a way to associate a unique output for each input of a specified type, for example, a real number or an element of a given set.

a. Coherent
b. Grill
c. Going up
d. Function

33. In mathematics, especially in the area of abstract algebra known as ring theory, a _____ is a ring with 0 ≠ 1 such that ab = 0 implies that either a = 0 or b = 0. That is, it is a nontrivial ring without left or right zero divisors. A commutative _____ is called an integral _____.

a. Left primitive ring
b. Modular representation theory
c. Domain
d. Simple ring

34. In descriptive statistics, the _____ is the length of the smallest interval which contains all the data. It is calculated by subtracting the smallest observations from the greatest and provides an indication of statistical dispersion.

It is measured in the same units as the data.

a. Kernel
b. Bandwidth
c. Class
d. Range

Chapter 3. Equations and Inequalities in Two Variables

35. _____ and independent variables refer to values that change in relationship to each other. The _____ are those that are observed to change in response to the independent variables. The independent variables are those that are deliberately manipulated to invoke a change in the _____.
   a. Round robin test
   b. Yates analysis
   c. Steiner system
   d. Dependent variables

36. Dependent variables and _____ refer to values that change in relationship to each other. The dependent variables are those that are observed to change in response to the _____. The _____ are those that are deliberately manipulated to invoke a change in the dependent variables.
   a. Experimental design diagram
   b. One-factor-at-a-time method
   c. Operational confound
   d. Independent variables

37. _____ is a term used in accounting, economics and finance to spread the cost of an asset over the span of several years.

   In simple words we can say that _____ is the reduction in the value of an asset due to usage, passage of time, wear and tear, technological outdating or obsolescence, depletion or other such factors.

   In accounting, _____ is a term used to describe any method of attributing the historical or purchase cost of an asset across its useful life, roughly corresponding to normal wear and tear.

   a. Depreciation
   b. 1-center problem
   c. Gross sales
   d. 120-cell

38. In mathematics, the _____ of a number n is the number that, when added to n, yields zero. The _____ of n is denoted −n. For example, 7 is −7, because 7 + (−7) = 0, and the _____ of −0.3 is 0.3, because −0.3 + 0.3 = 0.
   a. Additive inverse
   b. Associativity
   c. Algebraic structure
   d. Arity

Chapter 3. Equations and Inequalities in Two Variables

39. In cryptography, _____ is a pseudorandom number generator and a stream cipher designed by Robert Jenkins to be cryptographically secure. The name is an acronym for Indirection, Shift, Accumulate, Add, and Count.

The _____ algorithm has similarities with RC4.

   a. Imputation
   b. Isaac
   c. Order
   d. Introduction

40. The _____ (symbol: N) is the SI derived unit of force, named after Isaac _____ in recognition of his work on classical mechanics.

The _____ is the unit of force derived in the SI system; it is equal to the amount of force required to accelerate a mass of one kilogram at a rate of one meter per second per second. Algebraically:

$$1\ N = 1\ \frac{kg \cdot m}{s^2}.$$

- 1 N is the force of Earth's gravity on an object with a mass of about 102 g ($\frac{1}{9.8}$ kg) (such as a small apple.)
- On Earth's surface, a mass of 1 kg exerts a force of approximately 9.80665 N [down] (or 1 kgf.) The approximation of 1 kg corresponding to 10 N is sometimes used as a rule of thumb in everyday life and in engineering.
- The force of Earth's gravity on a human being with a mass of 70 kg is approximately 687 N.
- The dot product of force and distance is mechanical work. Thus, in SI units, a force of 1 N exerted over a distance of 1 m is 1 N·m of work. The Work-Energy Theorem states that the work done on a body is equal to the change in energy of the body. 1 N·m = 1 J (joule), the SI unit of energy.
- It is common to see forces expressed in kilonewtons or kN, where 1 kN = 1 000 N.

   a. 2-3 heap
   b. Newton
   c. 120-cell
   d. 1-center problem

Chapter 4. Systems of Linear Equations and Inequalities

1. A _____ is a mathematical model of a system based on the use of a linear operator. _____s typically exhibit features and properties that are much simpler than the general, nonlinear case. As a mathematical abstraction or idealization, _____s find important applications in automatic control theory, signal processing, and telecommunications.
    a. Hybrid system
    b. Predispositioning Theory
    c. Percolation
    d. Linear system

2. In mathematics, the _____ of a real number is its numerical value without regard to its sign. So, for example, 3 is the _____ of both 3 and −3.

   The _____ of a number a is denoted by $|a|$.

   Generalizations of the _____ for real numbers occur in a wide variety of mathematical settings.

    a. Absolute value
    b. A chemical equation
    c. Area hyperbolic functions
    d. A Mathematical Theory of Communication

3. In mathematics, an _____ is a statement about the relative size or order of two objects, or about whether they are the same or not

   - The notation a < b means that a is less than b.
   - The notation a > b means that a is greater than b.
   - The notation a ≠ b means that a is not equal to b, but does not say that one is bigger than the other or even that they can be compared in size.

   In all these cases, a is not equal to b, hence, '_____'.

   These relations are known as strict _____

   - The notation a ≤ b means that a is less than or equal to b;
   - The notation a ≥ b means that a is greater than or equal to b;

   An additional use of the notation is to show that one quantity is much greater than another, normally by several orders of magnitude.

   - The notation a << b means that a is much less than b.
   - The notation a >> b means that a is much greater than b.

Chapter 4. Systems of Linear Equations and Inequalities

If the sense of the _____ is the same for all values of the variables for which its members are defined, then the _____ is called an 'absolute' or 'unconditional' _____. If the sense of an _____ holds only for certain values of the variables involved, but is reversed or destroyed for other values of the variables, it is called a conditional _____.

An _____ may appear unsolvable because it only states whether a number is larger or smaller than another number; but it is possible to apply the same operations for equalities to inequalities. For example, to find x for the _____ 10x > 23 one would divide 23 by 10.

a. A posteriori
b. A chemical equation
c. A Mathematical Theory of Communication
d. Inequality

4. A _____ is an algebraic equation in which each term is either a constant or the product of a constant and a single variable. _____s can have one, two, three or more variables.

_____s occur with great regularity in applied mathematics.

a. Quartic equation
b. Linear equation
c. Difference of two squares
d. Quadratic equation

5. In quantum field theory and statistical mechanics in the thermodynamic limit, a system with a global symmetry can have more than one phase. For parameters where the symmetry is spontaneously broken, the system is said to be _____. When the global symmetry is unbroken the system is disordered.
   a. Ursell function
   b. Isoenthalpic-isobaric ensemble
   c. Einstein relation
   d. Ordered

6. Exponentiation is a mathematical operation, written a^n, involving two numbers, the base a and the _____ n. When n is a positive integer, exponentiation corresponds to repeated multiplication:

$$a^n = \underbrace{a \times \cdots \times a}_{n},$$

Chapter 4. Systems of Linear Equations and Inequalities

just as multiplication by a positive integer corresponds to repeated addition:

$$a \times n = \underbrace{a + \cdots + a}_{n}.$$

The _____ is usually shown as a superscript to the right of the base. The exponentiation a^n can be read as: a raised to the n-th power, a raised to the power [of] n or possibly a raised to the _____ [of] n, or more briefly: a to the n-th power or a to the power [of] n, or even more briefly: a to the n.

a. Exponential sum
b. Exponential tree
c. Exponentiating by squaring
d. Exponent

7. In algebra, a _____ is a function depending on n that associates a scalar, de, to every n×n square matrix A. The fundamental geometric meaning of a _____ is as the scale factor for measure when A is regarded as a linear transformation. _____s are important both in calculus, where they enter the substitution rule for several variables, and in multilinear algebra.

a. Determinant
b. Pfaffian
c. Functional determinant
d. 1-center problem

8. In linear algebra, a _____ of a matrix A is the determinant of some smaller square matrix, cut down from A by removing one or more of its rows or columns.

_____s obtained by removing just one row and one column from square matrices are required for calculating matrix cofactors, which in turn are useful for computing both the determinant and inverse of square matrices.

Let A be an m × n matrix and k an integer with 0 < k ≤ m, and k ≤ n.

a. Block size
b. Homogeneity
c. Minor
d. Chiral

Chapter 5. Exponents and Polynomials

39

1. In economics, business, retail, and accounting, a _____ is the value of money that has been used up to produce something, and hence is not available for use anymore. In business, the _____ may be one of acquisition, in which case the amount of money expended to acquire it is counted as _____. In this case, money is the input that is gone in order to acquire the thing.
   a. 2-3 heap
   b. 1-center problem
   c. 120-cell
   d. Cost

2. Exponentiation is a mathematical operation, written a^n, involving two numbers, the base a and the _____ n. When n is a positive integer, exponentiation corresponds to repeated multiplication:

$$a^n = \underbrace{a \times \cdots \times a}_{n},$$

just as multiplication by a positive integer corresponds to repeated addition:

$$a \times n = \underbrace{a + \cdots + a}_{n}.$$

The _____ is usually shown as a superscript to the right of the base. The exponentiation a^n can be read as: a raised to the n-th power, a raised to the power [of] n or possibly a raised to the _____ [of] n, or more briefly: a to the n-th power or a to the power [of] n, or even more briefly: a to the n.

   a. Exponential tree
   b. Exponentiating by squaring
   c. Exponential sum
   d. Exponent

3. The _____ are the set of numbers consisting of the natural numbers including 0 and their negatives. They are numbers that can be written without a fractional or decimal component, and fall within the set {... −2, −1, 0, 1, 2, ...}.
   a. Integers
   b. A Mathematical Theory of Communication
   c. A posteriori
   d. A chemical equation

4. _____, also sometimes known as standard form or as exponential notation, is a way of writing numbers that accommodates values too large or small to be conveniently written in standard decimal notation. _____ has a number of useful properties and is often favored by scientists, mathematicians and engineers, who work with such numbers.

In _____, numbers are written in the form:

$$a \times 10^b$$

   a. Scientific notation
   b. Radix point
   c. Leading zero
   d. 1-center problem

5. In elementary algebra, a _____ is a polynomial with two terms: the sum of two monomials. It is the simplest kind of polynomial except for a monomial.

The _____ $a^2 - b^2$ can be factored as the product of two other _____s:

   $a^2 - b^2$.

The product of a pair of linear _____s a x + b and c x + d is:

   2 +x + bd.

A _____ raised to the nth power, represented as

   n

can be expanded by means of the _____ theorem or, equivalently, using Pascal's triangle.

   a. Real structure
   b. Cylindrical algebraic decomposition
   c. Rational root theorem
   d. Binomial

6. In mathematics, a _____ is a constant multiplicative factor of a certain object. For example, in the expression $9x^2$, the _____ of x^2 is 9.

The object can be such things as a variable, a vector, a function, etc.

a. Multivariate division algorithm
b. Fibonacci polynomials
c. Coefficient
d. Stability radius

7. In mathematics, the word _____ means two different things in the context of polynomials:

- The first meaning is a product of powers of variables, or formally any value obtained from 1 by finitely many multiplications by a variable. If only a single variable x is considered this means that any _____ is either 1 or a power x^n of x, with n a positive integer. If several variables are considered, say, x, y, z, then each can be given an exponent, so that any _____ is of the form $x^a y^b z^c$ with a,b,c nonnegative integers.
- The second meaning of _____ includes _____s in the first sense, but also allows multiplication by any constant, so that − $7x^5$ and $4yz^{13}$ are also considered to be _____s.

With either definition, the set of _____s is a subset of all polynomials that is closed under multiplication.

a. Power sum symmetric polynomial
b. Diagonal form
c. Homogeneous polynomial
d. Monomial

8. In mathematics, a _____ is an expression constructed from variables and constants, using the operations of addition, subtraction, multiplication, and constant non-negative whole number exponents. For example, $x^2 − 4x + 7$ is a _____, but $x^2 − 4/x + 7x^{3/2}$ is not, because its second term involves division by the variable x and also because its third term contains an exponent that is not a whole number.

_____s are one of the most important concepts in algebra and throughout mathematics and science.

a. Coimage
b. Polynomial
c. Semifield
d. Group extension

9. In elementary algebra, a _____ is a polynomial consisting of three terms; in other words, a _____ is the sum of three monomials. It can be factored using simple steps

In linguistics, a _____ is a fixed expression which is made from three words; e.g. 'lights, camera, action', 'signed, sealed, delivered'.

Chapter 5. Exponents and Polynomials

a. Trinomial
b. Recurrence relation
c. Relation algebra
d. Symmetric difference

10. In linear algebra, two n-by-n matrices A and B over the field K are called _____ if there exists an invertible n-by-n matrix P over K such that

$$P^{-1}AP = B.$$

One of the meanings of the term similarity transformation is such a transformation of a matrix A into a matrix B.

Similarity is an equivalence relation on the space of square matrices.

_____ matrices share many properties:

- rank
- determinant
- trace
- eigenvalues
- characteristic polynomial
- minimal polynomial
- elementary divisors

There are two reasons for these facts:

- two _____ matrices can be thought of as describing the same linear map, but with respect to different bases
- the map $X \mapsto P^{-1}XP$ is an automorphism of the associative algebra of all n-by-n matrices, as the one-object case of the above category of all matrices.

Because of this, for a given matrix A, one is interested in finding a simple 'normal form' B which is _____ to A -- the study of A then reduces to the study of the simpler matrix B.

a. Similar
b. Dense
c. Coherence
d. Blinding

11. In mathematics, the _____s are an extension of the real numbers obtained by adjoining an imaginary unit, denoted i, which satisfies:

Chapter 5. Exponents and Polynomials

$$i^2 = -1.$$

Every _____ can be written in the form a + bi, where a and b are real numbers called the real part and the imaginary part of the _____, respectively.

_____s are a field, and thus have addition, subtraction, multiplication, and division operations. These operations extend the corresponding operations on real numbers, although with a number of additional elegant and useful properties, e.g., negative real numbers can be obtained by squaring _____s.

a. 1-center problem
b. Complex number
c. 120-cell
d. Real part

12. The mathematical concept of a _____ expresses the intuitive idea of deterministic dependence between two quantities, one of which is viewed as primary and the other as secondary. A _____ then is a way to associate a unique output for each input of a specified type, for example, a real number or an element of a given set.
a. Grill
b. Going up
c. Function
d. Coherent

13. _____ is the mathematical operation of scaling one number by another. It is one of the four basic operations in elementary arithmetic.

_____ is defined for whole numbers in terms of repeated addition; for example, 4 multiplied by 3 can be calculated by adding 3 copies of 4 together:

$$4 + 4 + 4 = 12.$$

_____ of rational numbers and real numbers is defined by systematic generalization of this basic idea.

a. Least common multiple
b. Multiplication
c. Highest common factor
d. The number 0 is even.

Chapter 5. Exponents and Polynomials

14. In mathematics, the _____ is when a number is squared and is then subtracted from another squared number. It refers to the identity

$$a^2 - b^2 = (a+b)(a-b)$$

from elementary algebra.

The proof is straightforward, starting from the RHS: apply the distributive law to get a sum of four terms, and set

$$ba - ab = 0$$

as an application of the commutative law.

  a. Linear equation
  b. Quartic equation
  c. Difference of two squares
  d. Quadratic equation

15. In mathematics, in the realm of group theory, a group is said to be _____ if it equals its own commutator subgroup if the group has no nontrivial abelian quotients.

The smallest _____ group is the alternating group A_5. More generally, any non-abelian simple group is _____ since the commutator subgroup is a normal subgroup with abelian quotient.

  a. Quaternion group
  b. Group of Lie type
  c. Perfect
  d. Free product

16. In mathematics, the _____ of a polynomial is the term of degree 0. For example, in the polynomial

X³ + 2X + 3

over the variable X, the _____ is 3. Here, the _____ is given by a numeral, but it may also be specified by a letter that is a parameter rather than a variable, as in the polynomial

ax² + bx + c,

in the variable x, where a, b, and c are parameters so that c is the _____.

a. Constant term
b. Jacobian conjecture
c. Sheffer sequence
d. Stability radius

17. In mathematics, a _____ is a polynomial equation of the second degree. The general form is

$$ax^2 + bx + c = 0,$$

where a ≠ 0.

The letters a, b, and c are called coefficients: the quadratic coefficient a is the coefficient of x^2, the linear coefficient b is the coefficient of x, and c is the constant coefficient, also called the free term or constant term.

a. Difference of two squares
b. Linear equation
c. Quartic equation
d. Quadratic equation

18. In mathematics, the _____ of a real number is its numerical value without regard to its sign. So, for example, 3 is the _____ of both 3 and −3.

The _____ of a number a is denoted by $|a|$.

Generalizations of the _____ for real numbers occur in a wide variety of mathematical settings.

a. A Mathematical Theory of Communication
b. Absolute value
c. A chemical equation
d. Area hyperbolic functions

19. A _____ is the longest side of a right triangle, the side opposite of the right angle. The length of the _____ of a right triangle can be found using the Pythagorean theorem, which states that the square of the length of the _____ equals the sum of the squares of the lengths of the two other sides.

For example, if one of the other sides has a length of 3 meters and the other has a length of 4 m.

Chapter 5. Exponents and Polynomials

a. Concyclic points
b. Reflection symmetry
c. Golden angle
d. Hypotenuse

20. In a right triangle, the cathetusoriginally from the Greek word KÎ¬θετος, plural catheti

- 1 Generally
- 2 References
- 3 See also
- 4 External links

In a wider sense, a _____ is any line falling perpendicularly on another line or a surface. Such a line is more commonly known as a surface normal.

a. Face diagonal
b. Central angle
c. Line segment
d. Cathetus

21. A _____ is one of the basic shapes of geometry: a polygon with three corners or vertices and three sides or edges which are line segments. A _____ with vertices A, B, and C is denoted ABC.

In Euclidean geometry any three non-collinear points determine a unique _____ and a unique plane.

a. 1-center problem
b. Kepler triangle
c. Fuhrmann circle
d. Triangle

Chapter 6. Rational Expressions and Rational Functions

1. In mathematics, an _____, or central tendency of a data set refers to a measure of the 'middle' or 'expected' value of the data set. There are many different descriptive statistics that can be chosen as a measurement of the central tendency of the data items.

An _____ is a single value that is meant to typify a list of values.

   a. A Mathematical Theory of Communication
   b. A chemical equation
   c. A posteriori
   d. Average

2. The mathematical concept of a _____ expresses the intuitive idea of deterministic dependence between two quantities, one of which is viewed as primary and the other as secondary. A _____ then is a way to associate a unique output for each input of a specified type, for example, a real number or an element of a given set.
   a. Going up
   b. Grill
   c. Coherent
   d. Function

3. In mathematics, a _____ is any function which can be written as the ratio of two polynomial functions. _____ of degree 2 :

$$y = \frac{x^2 - 3x - 2}{x^2 - 4}$$

In the case of one variable, x, a _____ is a function of the form

$$f(x) = \frac{P(x)}{Q(x)}$$

where P and Q are polynomial function in x and Q is not the zero polynomial. The domain of f is the set of all points x for which the denominator Q

   a. 1-center problem
   b. 120-cell
   c. Legendre rational functions
   d. Rational function

Chapter 6. Rational Expressions and Rational Functions

4. In mathematics, a _____ is an expression constructed from variables and constants, using the operations of addition, subtraction, multiplication, and constant non-negative whole number exponents. For example, $x^2 - 4x + 7$ is a _____, but $x^2 - 4/x + 7x^{3/2}$ is not, because its second term involves division by the variable x and also because its third term contains an exponent that is not a whole number.

_____s are one of the most important concepts in algebra and throughout mathematics and science.

a. Coimage
b. Semifield
c. Group extension
d. Polynomial

5. In mathematics, the _____s are an extension of the real numbers obtained by adjoining an imaginary unit, denoted i, which satisfies:

$$i^2 = -1.$$

Every _____ can be written in the form a + bi, where a and b are real numbers called the real part and the imaginary part of the _____, respectively.

_____s are a field, and thus have addition, subtraction, multiplication, and division operations. These operations extend the corresponding operations on real numbers, although with a number of additional elegant and useful properties, e.g., negative real numbers can be obtained by squaring _____s.

a. 120-cell
b. Real part
c. Complex number
d. 1-center problem

6. In algebra, _____ is an algorithm for dividing a polynomial by another polynomial of the same or lower degree, a generalised version of the familiar arithmetic technique called long division. It can be done easily by hand, because it separates an otherwise complex division problem into smaller ones.

For any polynomials f(x) and g(x), with g(x) not identical to zero, there exist unique polynomials q(x) and r(x) such that

$$\frac{f(x)}{g(x)} = q(x) + \frac{r(x)}{g(x)}$$

with r(x) having smaller degree than g(x.)

Chapter 6. Rational Expressions and Rational Functions

a. Square-free polynomial
b. Coefficient
c. Polynomial long division
d. Quadratic polynomial

7. In mathematics, a _____ is the end result of a division problem. It can also be expressed as the number of times the divisor divides into the dividend.
   a. Notation
   b. Marginal cost
   c. Quotient
   d. Limiting

8. In mathematics, a _____ is a statement that can be proved on the basis of explicitly stated or previously agreed assumptions.
   a. Disjunction introduction
   b. Theorem
   c. Boolean function
   d. Logical value

9. _____ is the mathematical operation of scaling one number by another. It is one of the four basic operations in elementary arithmetic.

_____ is defined for whole numbers in terms of repeated addition; for example, 4 multiplied by 3 can be calculated by adding 3 copies of 4 together:

$$4 + 4 + 4 = 12.$$

_____ of rational numbers and real numbers is defined by systematic generalization of this basic idea.

   a. The number 0 is even.
   b. Highest common factor
   c. Least common multiple
   d. Multiplication

10. In elementary algebra, a _____ is a polynomial with two terms: the sum of two monomials. It is the simplest kind of polynomial except for a monomial.

Chapter 6. Rational Expressions and Rational Functions

The _____ $a^2 - b^2$ can be factored as the product of two other _____s:

$a^2 - b^2$.

The product of a pair of linear _____s $ax + b$ and $cx + d$ is:

$2 + x + bd$.

A _____ raised to the nth power, represented as

n

can be expanded by means of the _____ theorem or, equivalently, using Pascal's triangle.

a. Real structure
b. Cylindrical algebraic decomposition
c. Rational root theorem
d. Binomial

11. In mathematics, the _____ or least common denominator is the least common multiple of the denominators of a set of vulgar fractions. It is the smallest positive integer that is a multiple of the denominators. For instance, the _____ of

$$\left\{\frac{5}{12}, \frac{11}{18}\right\}$$

is 36 because the least common multiple of 12 and 18 is 36.

a. Subtrahend
b. The number 0 is even.
c. Lowest common denominator
d. Highest common factor

12. The _____, named after Christian Doppler, is the change in frequency and wavelength of a wave for an observer moving relative to the source of the waves. It is commonly heard when a vehicle sounding a siren approaches, passes and recedes from an observer. The received frequency is increased during the approach, it is identical at the instant of passing by, and it is decreased during the recession.

a. 2-3 heap
b. 120-cell
c. 1-center problem
d. Doppler effect

13. In mathematics, the _____ of a real number is its numerical value without regard to its sign. So, for example, 3 is the _____ of both 3 and −3.

The _____ of a number a is denoted by | a |.

Generalizations of the _____ for real numbers occur in a wide variety of mathematical settings.

a. Absolute value
b. A chemical equation
c. Area hyperbolic functions
d. A Mathematical Theory of Communication

Chapter 7. Rational Exponents and Roots

1. In mathematics, a _____ of a number x is a number r such that r^2 = x, or, in other words, a number r whose square is x. Every non-negative real number x has a unique non-negative _____, called the principal _____, which is denoted with a radical symbol as $\sqrt{x}$, or, using exponent notation, as $x^{1/2}$. For example, the principal _____ of 9 is 3, denoted $\sqrt{9}$ = 3, because 3^2 = 3 × 3 = 9.
    a. Square root
    b. Double exponential
    c. Hyperbolic functions
    d. Multiplicative inverse

2. In geometry, a _____ is defined as a quadrilateral where all four of its angles are right angles.
    a. Cantor-Dedekind axiom
    b. Point group in two dimensions
    c. Rectangle
    d. Polytope

3. In vascular plants, the _____ is the organ of a plant body that typically lies below the surface of the soil. This is not always the case, however, since a _____ can also be aerial (that is, growing above the ground) or aerating (that is, growing up above the ground or especially above water.) Furthermore, a stem normally occurring below ground is not exceptional either
    a. 2-3 heap
    b. 120-cell
    c. 1-center problem
    d. Root

4. A _____ of a number is a number a such that a^3 = x.
    a. Golden function
    b. Hyperbolic functions
    c. Square root
    d. Cube root

5. In mathematics, an algebraic group G contains a unique maximal normal solvable subgroup; and this subgroup is closed. Its identity component is called the _____ of G.
    a. Composite
    b. Block size
    c. Barycentric coordinates
    d. Radical

Chapter 7. Rational Exponents and Roots

6. A _____ is an expression containing a square root.
   a. Convolution
   b. Controlled Cryptographic Item
   c. Convolution theorem
   d. Radical expression

7. Exponentiation is a mathematical operation, written a^n, involving two numbers, the base a and the _____ n. When n is a positive integer, exponentiation corresponds to repeated multiplication:

$$a^n = \underbrace{a \times \cdots \times a}_{n},$$

just as multiplication by a positive integer corresponds to repeated addition:

$$a \times n = \underbrace{a + \cdots + a}_{n}.$$

The _____ is usually shown as a superscript to the right of the base. The exponentiation a^n can be read as: a raised to the n-th power, a raised to the power [of] n or possibly a raised to the _____ [of] n, or more briefly: a to the n-th power or a to the power [of] n, or even more briefly: a to the n.

   a. Exponent
   b. Exponentiating by squaring
   c. Exponential sum
   d. Exponential tree

8. In mathematics and the arts, two quantities are in the _____ if the ratio between the sum of those quantities and the larger one is the same as the ratio between the larger one and the smaller. The _____ is an irrational mathematical constant, approximately 1.6180339887.

At least since the Renaissance, many artists and architects have proportioned their works to approximate the _____ -- especially in the form of the golden rectangle, in which the ratio of the longer side to the shorter is the _____ --believing this proportion to be aesthetically pleasing.

   a. 120-cell
   b. Golden ratio
   c. 1-center problem
   d. 2-3 heap

Chapter 7. Rational Exponents and Roots

9. In mathematics, a _____ is a curve which emanates from a central point, getting progressively farther away as it revolves around the point. An Archimedean _____, a helix, and a conic _____.

A '_____' and a 'helix' are two terms that are easily confused, but represent different objects.

A _____ is typically a planar curve, like the groove on a record or the arms of a _____ galaxy.

  a. Cornu spiral
  b. Logarithmic spiral
  c. Fresnel integrals
  d. Spiral

10. In linear algebra, two n-by-n matrices A and B over the field K are called _____ if there exists an invertible n-by-n matrix P over K such that

$$P^{-1}AP = B.$$

One of the meanings of the term similarity transformation is such a transformation of a matrix A into a matrix B.

Similarity is an equivalence relation on the space of square matrices.

_____ matrices share many properties:

- rank
- determinant
- trace
- eigenvalues
- characteristic polynomial
- minimal polynomial
- elementary divisors

There are two reasons for these facts:

- two _____ matrices can be thought of as describing the same linear map, but with respect to different bases
- the map $X \mapsto P^{-1}XP$ is an automorphism of the associative algebra of all n-by-n matrices, as the one-object case of the above category of all matrices.

Because of this, for a given matrix A, one is interested in finding a simple 'normal form' B which is _____ to A -- the study of A then reduces to the study of the simpler matrix B.

Chapter 7. Rational Exponents and Roots

a. Dense
b. Coherence
c. Similar
d. Blinding

11. In mathematics, the _____s are an extension of the real numbers obtained by adjoining an imaginary unit, denoted i, which satisfies:

$$i^2 = -1.$$

Every _____ can be written in the form a + bi, where a and b are real numbers called the real part and the imaginary part of the _____, respectively.

_____s are a field, and thus have addition, subtraction, multiplication, and division operations. These operations extend the corresponding operations on real numbers, although with a number of additional elegant and useful properties, e.g., negative real numbers can be obtained by squaring _____s.

a. 1-center problem
b. 120-cell
c. Real part
d. Complex number

12. _____ is the mathematical operation of scaling one number by another. It is one of the four basic operations in elementary arithmetic.

_____ is defined for whole numbers in terms of repeated addition; for example, 4 multiplied by 3 can be calculated by adding 3 copies of 4 together:

$$4 + 4 + 4 = 12.$$

_____ of rational numbers and real numbers is defined by systematic generalization of this basic idea.

a. Multiplication
b. Least common multiple
c. The number 0 is even.
d. Highest common factor

13. In elementary algebra, a _____ is a polynomial with two terms: the sum of two monomials. It is the simplest kind of polynomial except for a monomial.

Chapter 7. Rational Exponents and Roots

The _____ $a^2 - b^2$ can be factored as the product of two other _____s:

$a^2 - b^2$.

The product of a pair of linear _____s a x + b and c x + d is:

2 +x + bd.

A _____ raised to the nth power, represented as

n

can be expanded by means of the _____ theorem or, equivalently, using Pascal's triangle.

a. Rational root theorem
b. Real structure
c. Binomial
d. Cylindrical algebraic decomposition

14. In algebra, a _____ of an element in a quadratic extension field of a field K is its image under the unique non-identity automorphism of the extended field that fixes K. If the extension is generated by a square root of an element r of K, then the _____ of $a + b\sqrt{r}$ is $a - b\sqrt{r}$ for $a, b \in K$, and in particular in the case of the field C of complex numbers as an extension of the field R of real numbers, the complex _____ of a + bi is a − bi.

Forming the sum or product of any element of the extension field with its _____ always gives an element of K.

a. Relation algebra
b. Real structure
c. Trinomial
d. Conjugate

15. In mathematics, the _____ of a real number is its numerical value without regard to its sign. So, for example, 3 is the _____ of both 3 and −3.

The _____ of a number a is denoted by $|a|$.

Generalizations of the _____ for real numbers occur in a wide variety of mathematical settings.

Chapter 7. Rational Exponents and Roots

a. A chemical equation
b. Area hyperbolic functions
c. A Mathematical Theory of Communication
d. Absolute value

16. In mathematics, an _____ is a complex number whose squared value is a real number less than or equal to zero. The imaginary unit, denoted by i or j, is an example of an _____. If y is a real number, then iÂ·y is an _____, because:

$$(i \cdot y)^2 = i^2 \cdot y^2 = -y^2 \leq 0.$$

They were defined in 1572 by Rafael Bombelli.

a. A Mathematical Theory of Communication
b. A posteriori
c. A chemical equation
d. Imaginary number

17. In mathematics, the _____ of a complex number z, is the second element of the ordered pair of real numbers representing z,. It is denoted by Im or $\Im\{z\}$, where $\Im$ is a capital I in the Fraktur typeface. The complex function which maps z to the _____ of z is not holomorphic.
a. A posteriori
b. A Mathematical Theory of Communication
c. A chemical equation
d. Imaginary part

18. In mathematics, the _____ of a complex number z, is the first element of the ordered pair of real numbers representing z. It is denoted by Re{z} or $\Re\{z\}$, where $\Re$ is a capital R in the Fraktur typeface. The complex function which maps z to the _____ of z is not holomorphic.
a. 120-cell
b. 1-center problem
c. Complex number
d. Real part

19. _____, also sometimes known as standard form or as exponential notation, is a way of writing numbers that accommodates values too large or small to be conveniently written in standard decimal notation. _____ has a number of useful properties and is often favored by scientists, mathematicians and engineers, who work with such numbers.

Chapter 7. Rational Exponents and Roots

In _____, numbers are written in the form:

$$a \times 10^b$$

a. 1-center problem
b. Radix point
c. Leading zero
d. Scientific notation

20. In mathematics, the _____ of a complex number is given by changing the sign of the imaginary part. Thus, the conjugate of the complex number

$$z = a + ib$$

(where a and b are real numbers) is

$$\bar{z} = a - ib.$$

The _____ is also very commonly denoted by z*. Here $\bar{z}$ is chosen to avoid confusion with the notation for the conjugate transpose of a matrix (which can be thought of as a generalization of complex conjugation.)

a. 120-cell
b. 1-center problem
c. Real part
d. Complex conjugate

Chapter 8. Quadratic Functions

1. _____ is an algebraic technique used to solve quadratic equations, in analytic geometry for determining the shapes of graphs, and in calculus for computing integrals. The essential objective is to reduce a quadratic polynomial in a variable in an equation or expression to a squared polynomial of linear order. This can reduce an equation or integral to one that is more easily solved or evaluated.

    a. Permanent of a matrix
    b. Completing the square
    c. Monomial basis
    d. Relation algebra

2. In mathematics, a _____ is a polynomial equation of the second degree. The general form is

$$ax^2 + bx + c = 0,$$

where a ≠ 0.

The letters a, b, and c are called coefficients: the quadratic coefficient a is the coefficient of x^2, the linear coefficient b is the coefficient of x, and c is the constant coefficient, also called the free term or constant term.

    a. Quartic equation
    b. Difference of two squares
    c. Linear equation
    d. Quadratic equation

3. In mathematics, the _____ of a real number is its numerical value without regard to its sign. So, for example, 3 is the _____ of both 3 and −3.

The _____ of a number a is denoted by $|a|$.

Generalizations of the _____ for real numbers occur in a wide variety of mathematical settings.

    a. Area hyperbolic functions
    b. A chemical equation
    c. A Mathematical Theory of Communication
    d. Absolute value

4. In mathematics, a _____ is a statement that can be proved on the basis of explicitly stated or previously agreed assumptions.

a. Logical value
b. Theorem
c. Disjunction introduction
d. Boolean function

5. In computer science an _____ is a data structure consisting of a group of elements that are accessed by indexing. In most programming languages each element has the same data type and the _____ occupies a contiguous area of storage.

Most programming languages have a built-in _____ data type, although what is called an _____ in the language documentation is sometimes really an associative _____.

a. A posteriori
b. A chemical equation
c. Array
d. A Mathematical Theory of Communication

6. In algebra, a _____ is a function depending on n that associates a scalar, de, to every n×n square matrix A. The fundamental geometric meaning of a _____ is as the scale factor for measure when A is regarded as a linear transformation. _____s are important both in calculus, where they enter the substitution rule for several variables, and in multilinear algebra.

a. 1-center problem
b. Pfaffian
c. Functional determinant
d. Determinant

7. A quadratic equation with real solutions, called roots, which may be real or complex, is given by the _____: $x = \frac{-b \pm \sqrt{b^2 - 4ac}}{2a}$.

a. Parametric continuity
b. Differential Algebra
c. Quotient
d. Quadratic formula

8. In mathematics and in the sciences, a _____ (plural: _____e, formulæ or _____s) is a concise way of expressing information symbolically (as in a mathematical or chemical _____), or a general relationship between quantities. One of many famous _____e is Albert Einstein's $E = mc^2$ (see special relativity

Chapter 8. Quadratic Functions

In mathematics, a _____ is a key to solve an equation with variables. For example, the problem of determining the volume of a sphere is one that requires a significant amount of integral calculus to solve.

a. 2-3 heap
b. 1-center problem
c. Formula
d. 120-cell

9. In algebra, the _____ of a polynomial with real or complex coefficients is a certain expression in the coefficients of the polynomial which is equal to zero if and only if the polynomial has a multiple root in the complex numbers. For example, the _____ of the quadratic polynomial

$$ax^2 + bx + c$$ is $$b^2 - 4ac.$$

The _____ of the cubic polynomial

$$ax^3 + bx^2 + cx + d$$ is $$b^2c^2 - 4ac^3 - 4b^3d - 27a^2d^2 + 18abcd.$$

a. Discriminant
b. Jacobian conjecture
c. Boubaker polynomial
d. Square-free polynomial

10. In mathematics and the arts, two quantities are in the _____ if the ratio between the sum of those quantities and the larger one is the same as the ratio between the larger one and the smaller. The _____ is an irrational mathematical constant, approximately 1.6180339887.

At least since the Renaissance, many artists and architects have proportioned their works to approximate the _____ -- especially in the form of the golden rectangle, in which the ratio of the longer side to the shorter is the _____ --believing this proportion to be aesthetically pleasing.

a. 2-3 heap
b. 120-cell
c. 1-center problem
d. Golden ratio

11. In mathematics, the _____ is a conic section, the intersection of a right circular conical surface and a plane parallel to a generating straight line of that surface. Given a point and a line that lie in a plane, the locus of points in that plane that are equidistant to them is a _____.

A particular case arises when the plane is tangent to the conical surface of a circle.

   a. Directrix
   b. Dandelin sphere
   c. Parabola
   d. Matrix representation of conic sections

12. In geometry, a _____ is a special kind of point, usually a corner of a polygon, polyhedron, or higher dimensional polytope. In the geometry of curves a _____ is a point of where the first derivative of curvature is zero. In graph theory, a _____ is the fundamental unit out of which graphs are formed
   a. Crib
   b. Dini
   c. Duality
   d. Vertex

13. A _____ is a simple shape of Euclidean geometry consisting of those points in a plane which are at a constant distance, called the radius, from a fixed point, called the center. A _____ with center A is sometimes denoted by the symbol A.

A chord of a _____ is a line segment whose two endpoints lie on the _____.

   a. Circle
   b. Malfatti circles
   c. Circumcircle
   d. Circular segment

14. In mathematics, an _____ is a statement about the relative size or order of two objects, or about whether they are the same or not

   • The notation a < b means that a is less than b.
   • The notation a > b means that a is greater than b.
   • The notation a ≠ b means that a is not equal to b, but does not say that one is bigger than the other or even that they can be compared in size.

In all these cases, a is not equal to b, hence, '_____'.

Chapter 8. Quadratic Functions

These relations are known as strict _____

- The notation a ≤ b means that a is less than or equal to b;
- The notation a ≥ b means that a is greater than or equal to b;

An additional use of the notation is to show that one quantity is much greater than another, normally by several orders of magnitude.

- The notation a << b means that a is much less than b.
- The notation a >> b means that a is much greater than b.

If the sense of the _____ is the same for all values of the variables for which its members are defined, then the _____ is called an 'absolute' or 'unconditional' _____. If the sense of an _____ holds only for certain values of the variables involved, but is reversed or destroyed for other values of the variables, it is called a conditional _____.

An _____ may appear unsolvable because it only states whether a number is larger or smaller than another number; but it is possible to apply the same operations for equalities to inequalities. For example, to find x for the _____ 10x > 23 one would divide 23 by 10.

a. A posteriori
b. A chemical equation
c. A Mathematical Theory of Communication
d. Inequality

15. The _____ of any solid, plasma, vacuum or theoretical object is how much three-dimensional space it occupies, often quantified numerically. One-dimensional figures and two-dimensional shapes are assigned zero _____ in the three-dimensional space. _____ is presented as ml or cm³.

_____s of straight-edged and circular shapes are calculated using arithmetic formulae.

a. Cauchy momentum equation
b. Volume
c. Thermodynamic limit
d. Stress-energy tensor

Chapter 9. Exponential and Logarithmic Functions

1. The _____ of a quantity whose value decreases with time is the interval required for the quantity to decay to half of its initial value. The concept originated in describing how long it takes atoms to undergo radioactive decay, but also applies in a wide variety of other situations.

The term '_____' dates to 1907.

   a. Half-life
   b. Radioactive decay
   c. 120-cell
   d. 1-center problem

2. The _____ is a function in mathematics. The application of this function to a value x is written as ex. Equivalently, this can be written in the form e^x, where e is a mathematical constant, the base of the natural logarithm, which equals approximately 2.718281828, and is also known as Euler's number.
   a. Area hyperbolic functions
   b. A Mathematical Theory of Communication
   c. A chemical equation
   d. Exponential function

3. The mathematical concept of a _____ expresses the intuitive idea of deterministic dependence between two quantities, one of which is viewed as primary and the other as secondary. A _____ then is a way to associate a unique output for each input of a specified type, for example, a real number or an element of a given set.
   a. Function
   b. Coherent
   c. Going up
   d. Grill

4. A _____ is a simple shape of Euclidean geometry consisting of those points in a plane which are at a constant distance, called the radius, from a fixed point, called the center. A _____ with center A is sometimes denoted by the symbol A.

A chord of a _____ is a line segment whose two endpoints lie on the _____.

   a. Circumcircle
   b. Circular segment
   c. Circle
   d. Malfatti circles

Chapter 9. Exponential and Logarithmic Functions

5. _____ is the concept of adding accumulated interest back to the principal, so that interest is earned on interest from that moment on. The act of declaring interest to be principal is called compounding. A loan, for example, may have its interest compounded every month: in this case, a loan with $100 principal and 1% interest per month would have a balance of $101 at the end of the first month.
   a. Net interest margin securities
   b. Compound interest
   c. Retained interest
   d. Net interest margin

6. _____ is a fee, paid on borrowed capital. Assets lent include money, shares, consumer goods through hire purchase, major assets such as aircraft, and even entire factories in finance lease arrangements. The _____ is calculated upon the value of the assets in the same manner as upon money.
   a. Interest
   b. A Mathematical Theory of Communication
   c. Interest sensitivity gap
   d. Interest expense

7. In mathematics, the _____ of a number n is the number that, when added to n, yields zero. The _____ of n is denoted −n. For example, 7 is −7, because 7 + (−7) = 0, and the _____ of −0.3 is 0.3, because −0.3 + 0.3 = 0.
   a. Additive inverse
   b. Associativity
   c. Algebraic structure
   d. Arity

8. An _____ is a function which does the reverse of a given function.
   a. Empty function
   b. A Mathematical Theory of Communication
   c. Inverse Function
   d. Empty set

9. In mathematics, the _____ is a test used to determine if a function is injective, surjective or bijective.

Chapter 9. Exponential and Logarithmic Functions

Suppose there is a function f : X → Y with a graph., and you have a horizontal line of X x Y :
$$y_0 \in Y, \{(x, y_0) : x \in X\} = (X \times y_0).$$

- If the function is injective, then it can be visualized as one whose graph is never intersected by any horizontal line more than once.
- Iff f is surjective any horizontal line will intersect the graph at least at one point
- If f is bijective any horizontal line will intersect the graph at exactly one point.

This test is also used to find whether or not the inverse of the function is indeed a function as well. This is due to the reflective properties of the function over y=x.

a. Subset
b. Multiset
c. Disjoint sets
d. Horizontal line test

10. An injective function is called an injection, and is also said to be a _____ (not to be confused with one-to-one correspondence, i.e. a bijective function.)

A function f that is not injective is sometimes called many-to-one. (However, this terminology is also sometimes used to mean 'single-valued', i.e. each argument is mapped to at most one value.)

a. One-to-one function
b. A chemical equation
c. A posteriori
d. A Mathematical Theory of Communication

11. Any formula written in terms of logarithms may be said to be in _____.

In contexts including complex manifolds and algebraic geometry, a logarithmic differential form is a 1-form that, locally at least, can be written

$$\frac{df}{f}$$

for some meromorphic function f. That is, for some open covering, there are local representations of this differential form as a logarithmic derivative.

Chapter 9. Exponential and Logarithmic Functions

a. Holomorphic sheaf
b. Cauchy-Hadamard theorem
c. Laurent series
d. Logarithmic form

12. The function $\log_b(x)$ depends on both b and x, but the term _____ (or logarithmic function) in standard usage refers to a function of the form $\log_b(x)$ in which the base b is fixed and so the only argument is x. Thus there is one _____ for each value of the base b (which must be positive and must differ from 1.) Viewed in this way, the base-b _____ is the inverse function of the exponential function b^x.

   a. 1-center problem
   b. Logarithm function
   c. 2-3 heap
   d. 120-cell

13. In mathematics, the _____ of a real number is its numerical value without regard to its sign. So, for example, 3 is the _____ of both 3 and −3.

The _____ of a number a is denoted by $|a|$.

Generalizations of the _____ for real numbers occur in a wide variety of mathematical settings.

   a. A chemical equation
   b. A Mathematical Theory of Communication
   c. Area hyperbolic functions
   d. Absolute value

14. In mathematics, the _____ of a number to a given base is the power or exponent to which the base must be raised in order to produce the number.

For example, the _____ of 1000 to the base 10 is 3, because 3 is how many 10s one must multiply to get 1000: thus 10 × 10 × 10 = 1000; the base-2 _____ of 32 is 5 because 5 is how many 2s one must multiply to get 32: thus 2 × 2 × 2 × 2 × 2 = 32. In the language of exponents: $10^3 = 1000$, so $\log_{10} 1000 = 3$, and $2^5 = 32$, so $\log_2 32 = 5$.

a. 1-center problem
b. Logarithm
c. 2-3 heap
d. 120-cell

15. The _____ is the logarithm with base 10. It is also known as the decadic logarithm, named after its base. It is indicated by $\log_{10}$
   a. Common logarithm
   b. 1-center problem
   c. Natural logarithm
   d. Logarithmic growth

16. The _____ function $\text{antilog}_b(y)$ is the inverse function of the logarithm function $\log_b(x)$; it can be written in closed form as b^y. The antilog notation was common before the advent of modern calculators and computers: tables of _____s to the base 10 were useful in carrying out computations by hand. The notation still appears in some modern books, and is still used in some situations.
   a. A chemical equation
   b. Antilogarithm
   c. A Mathematical Theory of Communication
   d. A posteriori

17. In mathematics, the _____ of a ring R, often denoted cha, is defined to be the smallest number of times one must add the ring's multiplicative identity element to itself to get the additive identity element; the ring is said to have _____ zero if this repeated sum never reaches the additive identity. That is, cha is the smallest positive number n such that

$$\underbrace{1 + \cdots + 1}_{n \text{ summands}} = 0$$

if such a number n exists, and 0 otherwise. The _____ may also be taken to be the exponent of the ring's additive group, that is, the smallest positive n such that

$$\underbrace{a + \cdots + a}_{n \text{ summands}} = 0$$

for every element a of the ring.

Chapter 9. Exponential and Logarithmic Functions

a. Class
b. Coherent
c. Disk
d. Characteristic

18. The _____, formerly known as the hyperbolic logarithm, is the logarithm to the base e, where e is an irrational constant approximately equal to 2.718 281 828. It is also sometimes referred to as the Napierian logarithm, although the original meaning of this term is slightly different. In simple terms, the _____ of a number x is the power to which e would have to be raised to equal x -- for example the natural log of e itself is 1 because e^1 = e, while the _____ of 1 would be 0, since e^0 = 1.
    a. Natural logarithm
    b. 1-center problem
    c. Logarithmic growth
    d. Logarithmic identities

19. The _____ is the period of time required for a quantity to double in size or value.
    a. Power law
    b. Stretched exponential function
    c. Zenzizenzizenzic
    d. Doubling time

20. In computational complexity theory, an algorithm is said to take _____ if the asymptotic upper bound for the time it requires is proportional to the size of the input, which is usually denoted n.

Informally spoken, the running time increases linearly with the size of the input. For example, a procedure that adds up all elements of a list requires time proportional to the length of the list.

   a. Time-constructible function
   b. Linear time
   c. Truth table reduction
   d. Constructible function

21. In mathematics and computer science, _____ (also base-16, hexa or base, of 16. It uses sixteen distinct symbols, most often the symbols 0-9 to represent values zero to nine, and A, B, C, D, E, F (or a through f) to represent values ten to fifteen.

Its primary use is as a human friendly representation of binary coded values, so it is often used in digital electronics and computer engineering.

a. Factoradic
b. Tetradecimal
c. Radix
d. Hexadecimal

22. _____ is a term used in accounting, economics and finance to spread the cost of an asset over the span of several years.

In simple words we can say that _____ is the reduction in the value of an asset due to usage, passage of time, wear and tear, technological outdating or obsolescence, depletion or other such factors.

In accounting, _____ is a term used to describe any method of attributing the historical or purchase cost of an asset across its useful life, roughly corresponding to normal wear and tear.

a. Gross sales
b. Depreciation
c. 120-cell
d. 1-center problem

Chapter 10. Conic Sections

1. In mathematics, a _____ is a curve obtained by intersecting a cone with a plane. A _____ is therefore a restriction of a quadric surface to the plane. The _____s were named and studied as long ago as 200 BC, when Apollonius of Perga undertook a systematic study of their properties.

   a. Conic section
   b. Directrix
   c. Dandelin sphere
   d. Parabola

2. In mathematics and in the sciences, a _____ (plural: _____e, formulæ or _____s) is a concise way of expressing information symbolically (as in a mathematical or chemical _____), or a general relationship between quantities. One of many famous _____e is Albert Einstein's E = mc² (see special relativity

   In mathematics, a _____ is a key to solve an equation with variables. For example, the problem of determining the volume of a sphere is one that requires a significant amount of integral calculus to solve.

   a. Formula
   b. 1-center problem
   c. 120-cell
   d. 2-3 heap

3. A _____ is a simple shape of Euclidean geometry consisting of those points in a plane which are at a constant distance, called the radius, from a fixed point, called the center. A _____ with center A is sometimes denoted by the symbol A.

   A chord of a _____ is a line segment whose two endpoints lie on the _____.

   a. Circular segment
   b. Malfatti circles
   c. Circumcircle
   d. Circle

4. In mathematics an _____ , a 'falling short') is a conic section, the locus of points in a plane such that the sum of the distances to two fixed points is equal to a given constant. The two fixed points are then called foci.

   Another way is to define it as the path traced out by a point whose distance from a focus maintains a constant ratio less than one with its distance from a straight line not passing through the focus, called the directrix.

a. A chemical equation
b. Ellipse
c. A Mathematical Theory of Communication
d. A posteriori

5. In mathematics, an _____ is a statement about the relative size or order of two objects, or about whether they are the same or not

- The notation a < b means that a is less than b.
- The notation a > b means that a is greater than b.
- The notation a ≠ b means that a is not equal to b, but does not say that one is bigger than the other or even that they can be compared in size.

In all these cases, a is not equal to b, hence, '_____'.

These relations are known as strict _____

- The notation a ≤ b means that a is less than or equal to b;
- The notation a ≥ b means that a is greater than or equal to b;

An additional use of the notation is to show that one quantity is much greater than another, normally by several orders of magnitude.

- The notation a << b means that a is much less than b.
- The notation a >> b means that a is much greater than b.

If the sense of the _____ is the same for all values of the variables for which its members are defined, then the _____ is called an 'absolute' or 'unconditional' _____. If the sense of an _____ holds only for certain values of the variables involved, but is reversed or destroyed for other values of the variables, it is called a conditional _____.

An _____ may appear unsolvable because it only states whether a number is larger or smaller than another number; but it is possible to apply the same operations for equalities to inequalities. For example, to find x for the _____ 10x > 23 one would divide 23 by 10.

a. A Mathematical Theory of Communication
b. Inequality
c. A posteriori
d. A chemical equation

Chapter 10. Conic Sections

6. In mathematics, the _____ of a real number is its numerical value without regard to its sign. So, for example, 3 is the _____ of both 3 and −3.

The _____ of a number a is denoted by $|a|$.

Generalizations of the _____ for real numbers occur in a wide variety of mathematical settings.

   a. A chemical equation
   b. A Mathematical Theory of Communication
   c. Area hyperbolic functions
   d. Absolute value

7. In mathematics, a _____ is a system which is not linear. Less technically, a _____ is any problem where the variabl to be solved for cannot be written as a linear sum of independent components. A nonhomogenous system, which is linear apart from the presence of a function of the independent variables, is nonlinear according to a strict definition, but such systems are usually studied alongside linear systems, because they can be transformed to a linear system as long as a particular solution is known.
   a. George Dantzig
   b. Nonlinear system
   c. Metric system
   d. 1-center problem

8. In propositional logic, contraposition is a logical relationship between two statements of material implication. A proposition Q is materially implied by a proposition P when the following relationship holds:

$$(P \rightarrow Q)$$

In vernacular terms, this states 'If P then Q', or, 'If Socrates is a man then Socrates is human.' In a conditional such as this, P is called the antecedent and Q the consequent. One statement is the _____ of the other just when its antecedent is the negated consequent of the other, and vice-versa.

   a. Continuous signal
   b. Control chart
   c. Contour map
   d. Contrapositive

9. In mathematics, the _____ of a number n is the number that, when added to n, yields zero. The _____ of n is denoted −n. For example, 7 is −7, because 7 + (−7) = 0, and the _____ of −0.3 is 0.3, because −0.3 + 0.3 = 0.

a. Associativity
b. Additive inverse
c. Algebraic structure
d. Arity

ANSWER KEY

Chapter 1
1. c   2. b   3. b   4. d   5. d   6. a   7. d   8. d   9. d   10. d
11. d   12. d   13. d   14. c   15. d   16. a   17. d   18. a   19. b   20. c
21. d   22. b   23. d   24. d   25. d   26. d   27. d   28. d   29. a   30. d
31. d   32. a   33. b   34. d   35. d   36. c   37. b   38. d   39. a   40. c
41. d   42. d   43. c   44. d   45. d   46. d   47. b   48. c   49. a   50. b
51. b

Chapter 2
1. d   2. d   3. d   4. d   5. d   6. a   7. c   8. a   9. d   10. d
11. d   12. a   13. d   14. a   15. d   16. a   17. b   18. b   19. a   20. d
21. d   22. c   23. d   24. b

Chapter 3
1. b   2. c   3. d   4. b   5. d   6. a   7. d   8. c   9. d   10. d
11. b   12. d   13. b   14. c   15. d   16. a   17. d   18. d   19. d   20. d
21. d   22. c   23. d   24. d   25. b   26. d   27. d   28. d   29. d   30. b
31. a   32. d   33. c   34. d   35. d   36. d   37. a   38. a   39. b   40. b

Chapter 4
1. d   2. a   3. d   4. b   5. d   6. d   7. a   8. c

Chapter 5
1. d   2. d   3. a   4. a   5. d   6. c   7. d   8. b   9. a   10. a
11. b   12. c   13. b   14. c   15. c   16. a   17. d   18. b   19. d   20. d
21. d

Chapter 6
1. d   2. d   3. d   4. d   5. c   6. c   7. c   8. b   9. d   10. d
11. c   12. d   13. a

Chapter 7
1. a   2. c   3. d   4. d   5. d   6. d   7. a   8. b   9. d   10. c
11. d   12. a   13. c   14. d   15. d   16. d   17. d   18. d   19. d   20. d

Chapter 8
1. b   2. d   3. d   4. b   5. c   6. d   7. d   8. c   9. a   10. d
11. c   12. d   13. a   14. d   15. b

Chapter 9
1. a   2. d   3. a   4. c   5. b   6. a   7. a   8. c   9. d   10. a
11. d   12. b   13. d   14. b   15. a   16. b   17. d   18. a   19. d   20. b
21. d   22. b

Chapter 10
1. a   2. a   3. d   4. b   5. b   6. d   7. b   8. d   9. b

www.ingramcontent.com/pod-product-compliance
Lightning Source LLC
Chambersburg PA
CBHW081849230426
43669CB00018B/2885